RON MILLER

EARTH AND THE MOON

WORLDS BEYOND

TWENTY-FIRST CENTURY BOOKS · BROOKFIELD, CONNECTICUT

This book is for Jordan Duvall.

Illustrations by Ron Miller. Photographs courtesy of NASA.

Library of Congress Cataloging-in-Publication Data
Miller, Ron, 1947–
Earth and the moon / Ron Miller.
p. cm. — (Worlds beyond)
Summary: Chronicles the origin, evolution, and exploration of the Earth and the Moon,
and discusses their composition, their place in our solar system, and more.
Includes bibliographical references and index.
ISBN 0-7613-2358-9
1. Earth—Juvenile literature. 2. Moon—Juvenile literature. [1. Earth. 2. Moon.] I. Title.
QB631.4 .M56 2002 525—dc21 2001008479

Published by Twenty-First Century Books
A Division of The Millbrook Press, Inc.
2 Old New Milford Road
Brookfield, Connecticut 06804
www.millbrookpress.com

Manufactured in China
5 4 3 2 1

CHAPTER ONE

DISCOVERING A PLANET

The ground beneath your feet is the surface of a planet. Earth is one of nine planets that make up the solar system. Ours is neither the largest planet nor the smallest. It is not the one closest to the Sun, nor is it the farthest away. It might seem at first glance to be a perfectly average planet, but it is in fact one of the most unusual.

To a visitor from another star, Earth might seem to have been misnamed, for the word *earth* simply means *dirt* or *land*. But the first thing an extraterrestrial visitor would notice about the beautiful blue planet is that it is mostly covered by *water*—with dry land accounting for only about one-quarter of its surface. It would have been much better named Ocean. This alone makes it unique among all the planets, for no others can boast open bodies of liquid water. Perhaps this is because they are so close to the Sun that water will boil away, or so far away that it is permanently frozen. Water makes possible many of the other unique features of planet Earth, not the least of which is you—the creature holding this book and reading these words—because without liquid water life might never have evolved on Earth.

There are two kinds of planets in the solar system, **gas giants** like Jupiter and Saturn, which are made almost entirely of gas and liquid, and **terrestrial planets**, which are made almost entirely of rock and metal. There are four terrestrial planets in the solar system: Mercury, Venus, Earth, and Mars. They are called terrestrial planets because they resemble Earth in their composition (*terra* is the Greek word for "earth"). Earth is the largest of the terrestrial planets.

Understanding how and why the other planets in the solar system resemble Earth, and how and why they might be different, helps us to better understand our own planet. It is much the same way that you understand your friends better if you know their brothers and sisters, mothers and fathers. Earth is also part of a family. It was born at the same time as the other planets in the solar system, and was formed from many of the same materials. Earth shares many features and qualities with its planetary brothers and sisters, like a family of nine children. And like a human family, some of the children may be nearly identical, such as Venus and Earth, while others may hardly resemble one another at all. But because they all share the same parentage, there are features common to them all.

Many people think of Earth today as being somehow "finished"—that all of its history led up to the world we see around us, and that is the end of it. But Earth is a dynamic planet. It is always changing. It has not always looked the way it does now, and it will not look the same in the future. What you see outside the windows of your home or school looked entirely different long ago. Millions of years ago it may have been the top of a mountain or the bottom of a sea. It may have been a thick jungle or a barren desert. Billions of years ago it was probably an ocean

Facing page: The four rocky terrestrial planets and the four gas giants of our solar system (Pluto is neither a gas giant nor a terrestrial planet. Most scientists believe it to be little more than a ball of dirty ice similar to Neptune's moon, Triton.)

TERRESTRIAL PLANETS

Mercury

Venus

Earth

Mars

GAS GIANTS

Neptune

Uranus

Jupiter

Saturn

MERCURY VENUS EARTH MARS JUPITER SATURN URANUS NEPTUNE PLUTO

A family portrait: the planets and moons of our solar system shown to the same scale as the Sun

of liquid rock. Likewise, what you see outside your window will not look the same a million or a billion years from now. We live in a small cross section of the history of Earth, located about halfway between its creation and the time an aging Sun will cause its end. There is a lot of history that led up to the Earth we know and a lot of future still ahead.

CHAPTER TWO

THE BEGINNING

There have been theories about the origin of the solar system ever since it was first realized that there *was* a solar system. This occurred in 1609, when the Italian scientist Galileo Galilei became the first person to look at the night sky with a telescope. Until then, the planets were thought to be merely a special class of stars that moved among the other stars (the word *planet* comes from a Greek word meaning "wanderer"). When Galileo chose to look at Venus, Mars, Saturn, and Jupiter he didn't expect to see anything special. What he discovered, however, was that Earth was not the only planet in the universe, that there were other worlds in space circling the Sun. He found that the "stars" called Jupiter, Venus, Saturn, and Mars were in fact other worlds, perhaps worlds much like his own.

In the four centuries since Galileo's discovery there have been many theories about the origin of the solar system and Earth. The currently accepted theory of the development of the solar system determined that the Sun and planets formed about 4.5 billion years ago from an enormous cloud of dust and gas. This can only happen if the cloud is large enough for the gravitation of its individual particles to start the cloud contracting and to keep the contraction going. But once this process began, the cloud shrank to a millionth of its original size very quickly. During this collapse, it became what is known as a **protostar**.

As more and more particles gathered in the center of the cloud, it became denser, and as it became denser its gravity increased. This, in turn, caused it to collapse even further. Soon the core began to heat up, glowing red within the dark cloud. The intense heat and pressure caused a nuclear reaction to begin—perhaps only a few thousand years after the cloud first began to condense. As soon as this happened, the protostar, in which no nuclear reactions take place, became a star, which is powered by nuclear reactions. The increased amount of heat produced created an outward pressure that resisted the collapsing dust and gas . . . and the collapse came to a halt. The Hubble Space Telescope has observed young solar systems in just this phase of development. Called **protoplanetary disks**, they look like dark, bun-shaped circles, often with a dimly glowing center.

Within the cloud, tiny particles of dust collided and stuck together, forming tiny clumps of material. As these clumps—called **planetesimals**—grew in size, they attracted more particles. This process is called **accretion**. Most of these early collisions were relatively gentle, so the planetesimals didn't knock themselves into pieces. Soon grains of dust grew to the size of rocks, then boulders, and then **asteroids** miles across. The whole process of growing from the size of a large pinhead to a mountain may have taken only 100,000 years or so. At this point the process began to

Earth and the rest of the solar system formed from a disk of gas and dust that surrounded the early Sun.

slow down—the original dust and gas were being used up, and the cloud grew thin. Several stars have been observed with large, thin disks of dust surrounding them—such as Beta Pictoris—which may be solar systems in this stage of development.

As the planetesimals grew larger they began to move faster, and the collisions between them became more violent. Instead of accreting, some of them shattered into pieces. The few planetesimals that were large enough to survive the collisions grew even larger, devouring the debris from the unluckier smaller objects. Once the process of accretion began, they grew very quickly. Earth may have gone from a cloud of dust to a body nearly its present size in as few as 40 million years.

The Birth of a Planet

The surface of Earth 4.5 billion years ago was covered by a **magma** ocean, a sea of **molten** rock tens of miles deep. Much of the heat that kept the surface molten came from the millions of **meteors** and asteroids that continually rained onto it. These impacts also broke up any crust as fast as it formed. The rate at which the early Earth was impacted was probably hundreds of millions of times greater than it is today because the solar system was still filled with debris left over from its creation. The smaller asteroids heated the surface, but the largest ones made **craters** more than 600 miles (966 km) wide and 25 to 60 miles (40 to 96 km) deep. The heat from these giant impacts was retained deep within Earth.

Earth was built up bit by bit by the accumulation of billions of planetesimals, or small chunks of rock and metal.

The early Earth was covered with a vast ocean of molten rock called magma.

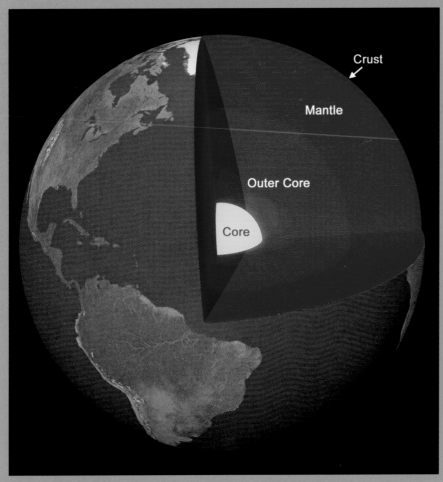

A cross section of Earth: The core and mantle together form the bulk of the planet. The outer crust on which we live is as thin, in comparison, as the skin of an apple.

If you could slice Earth in half you would see that it is formed of layers. At the center is a hot **core** that extends about halfway to the surface. This core is made mostly of nickel and iron. The outer part of the core is molten, but the inner part is solid due to the incredible pressures at the center of Earth.

Surrounding the core is a layer of dense rock called the **mantle**. The rock that makes up the mantle has more metal in it than the crust of Earth, but less metal than the core.

The crust of Earth—the part we walk around on—is a few tens of miles thick and is composed mostly of familiar materials, such as granite, basalt, and sedimentary rocks. The crust is thinnest beneath the oceans, where it is approximately only 4 miles (7 km) thick, but under the **continents** it averages about 25 miles (40 km) thick. Under mountain ranges, the crust may be 50 miles (80 km) thick. The continents are like huge rafts of low-density rock floating on the mantle.

Most of our knowledge of the interior of Earth comes from studying earthquakes. **Seismic** waves created by earthquakes pass through the planet. As they do so, they are affected by changes in the type of material in much the same way that light is bent when it passes from air to water or glass. By studying these changes, scientists have been able to deduce the different layers that exist far beneath our feet.

Although Earth has been bombarded by meteorites, erosion has erased most of them. Meteor Crater in Arizona still exists because it was created only 20,000–40,000 years ago. It is nearly a mile (1.6 km) across and was formed by the impact of a body 150 feet (45.7 m) wide, weighing 300,000 tons. [NASA]

The outer surface of Earth was so hot that all of the iron it contained was molten. It's possible that the mantle itself was molten as well. The heavy, molten metal separated itself from the surrounding rock and began to drain toward the core of the planet. (Modern steel mills separate iron ore from its impurities by using a similar process. As the iron melts it sinks toward the bottom of the smelter while the silicate-rich rocky slag, which is lighter than the metal, floats on top.) This lighter material, left behind by the iron, eventually became Earth's crust.

The number of meteor impacts decreased as the amount of leftover material in the solar system got used up. Since there were fewer impacts, the surface of Earth began to cool. As it did, liquid water began to collect on its surface. Most of this was released from the minerals that made up the crust and mantle, but a great deal might also have been added by the impact of icy asteroids—**comets**—from the outer solar system.

Earth would have continued with its cooling in peace and quiet—eventually becoming a planet perhaps only a little larger than Mars is today—had not something extraordinary happened to it, something so catastrophic that Earth was nearly destroyed. This is the story of where the Moon came from.

CHAPTER THREE
THE STORY OF THE MOON

There have been nearly as many theories attempting to account for the origin of the Moon as there have been about the origin of Earth. It was not until the Apollo astronauts brought back actual samples of the Moon that scientists learned exactly what the Moon is made of and how old it is. Beginning in 1975, several astronomers began developing the idea that the Moon might have been created when an object the size of Mars hit Earth more than 4 billion years ago, when our planet was still mostly molten. This titanic collision flung the raw ingredients for the Moon into **orbit** around Earth, like the rings around Saturn.

Astronomer William K. Hartmann, one of the originators of the **impact hypothesis**, realized that some of the huge impact craters on the Moon must have been made by objects as large as 90 miles (145 km) across. He reasoned that in the distant past there must have been objects at least ten times larger than these—perhaps as large as the planet Mars. If one of these objects had hit Earth, Hartmann and his colleague Donald Davis thought, enough material from the collision might have been blown into orbit to have formed the Moon.

The collision probably took place when Earth was only about half formed. The impact threw a ring of very hot debris into orbit

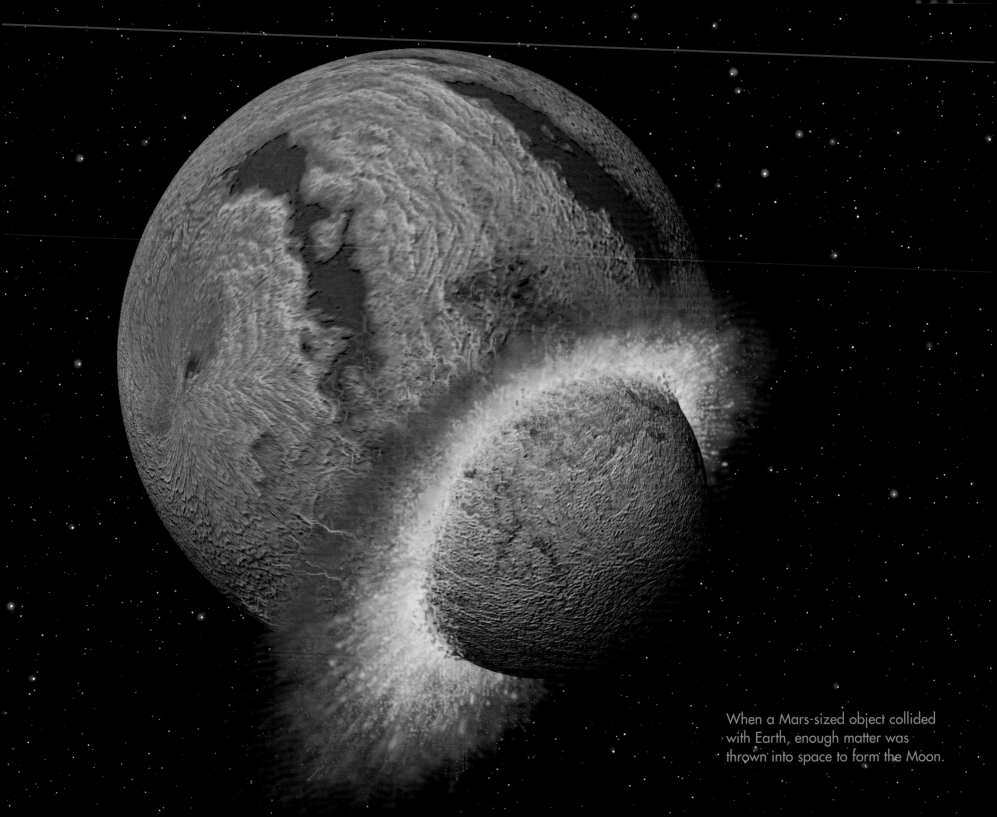

When a Mars-sized object collided with Earth, enough matter was thrown into space to form the Moon.

Earth as seen from the Moon, shortly after the Moon's formation: Earth is still surrounded by the ring of debris left over from the impact that created the Moon.

around the young Earth. The Moon probably formed by accretion very quickly from this debris, perhaps in fewer than ten years.

The Moon would have been very hot—probably molten—when it formed. This theory is supported by the Clementine lunar orbiter, which recently discovered that the Moon was once covered by molten **lava**. The Moon probably continued to accrete material. These impacts kept the magma ocean molten and broke up any crust that happened to form.

The newly formed Moon began to gradually spiral farther and farther away from Earth. One hundred million years after its creation—4.4 billion years ago—the Moon was already halfway to its present distance.

In the seventeenth century German astronomer Johannes Kepler discovered that the closer a moon is to a planet the faster it moves in its orbit, and the farther away it is, the slower it moves. If the Moon were farther away from Earth, it would move more slowly. Likewise, if the Moon slowed down, it would compensate by moving farther away. As the Moon orbits Earth, the gravity of Earth pulls on the Moon. One result of this is that Earth slows the Moon down. As it moves more slowly, the Moon moves away from Earth a tiny amount every year.

The drag of the Moon's pull has also been slowing down the rotation of Earth. Shortly after the formation of the Moon, Earth's day was only five or six hours long. It has been growing longer ever since, though only by a few fractions of a second every year.

CHAPTER FOUR

EARTH, AIR, FIRE, AND WATER

Asteroids continued to bombard Earth after the formation of the Moon, but the impacts gradually became smaller and less violent as the area of space surrounding Earth's orbit was gradually cleared of debris. Since fewer impacts were taking place, a thick crust began to form over Earth's semi-molten mantle. Volcanoes erupted everywhere, pouring vast quantities of gases into the thin atmosphere. The ash and smoke from the volcanoes, combined with the dust blown into the sky by the continuing impacts, kept the atmosphere opaque and gloomy. The landscape would have been lit only by the dim red glow from the cooling magma ocean. The huge nearby Moon would have been visible only rarely through the dense cloud cover, as would the Sun, which was not as yet as bright as it is today. The Sun and the Moon would have rushed through Earth's sky more than twice as fast as they do today, since Earth was rotating much faster—in ten hours instead of twenty-four.

This early atmosphere had little or no oxygen in it. Instead, it was probably composed mostly of hydrogen, the gas most com-

TIMELINE OF EARTH'S HISTORY

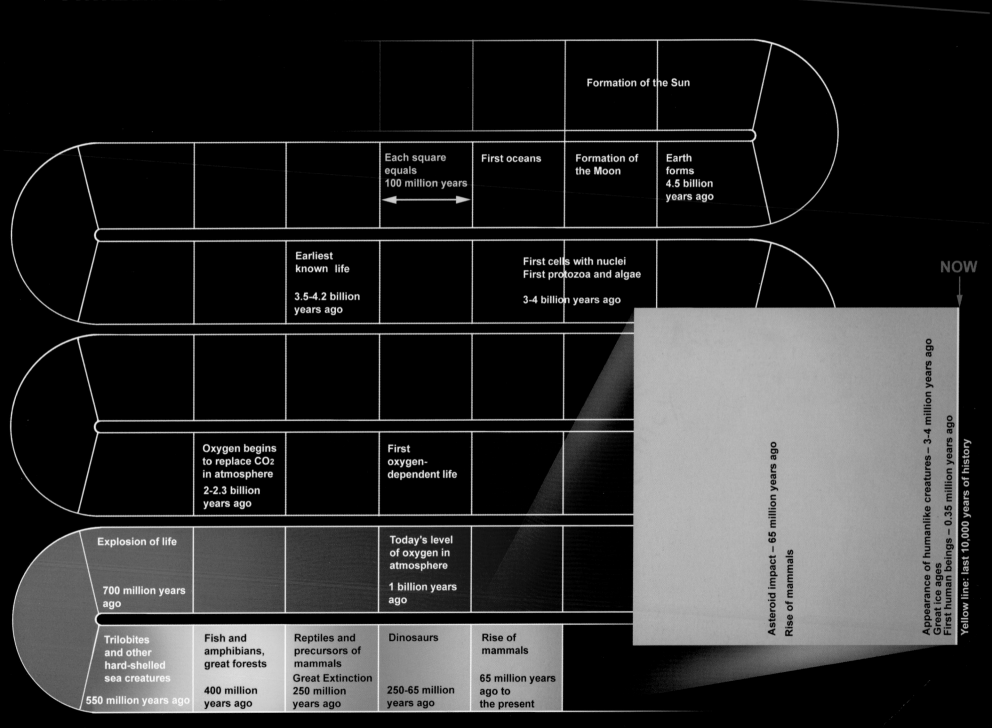

Formation of the Sun

Each square equals 100 million years

First oceans

Formation of the Moon

Earth forms 4.5 billion years ago

Earliest known life

3.5-4.2 billion years ago

First cells with nuclei
First protozoa and algae

3-4 billion years ago

NOW

Oxygen begins to replace CO₂ in atmosphere

2-2.3 billion years ago

First oxygen-dependent life

Explosion of life

700 million years ago

Today's level of oxygen in atmosphere

1 billion years ago

Trilobites and other hard-shelled sea creatures

550 million years ago

Fish and amphibians, great forests

400 million years ago

Reptiles and precursors of mammals

Great Extinction 250 million years ago

Dinosaurs

250-65 million years ago

Rise of mammals

65 million years ago to the present

Asteroid impact – 65 million years ago
Rise of mammals

Appearance of humanlike creatures – 3-4 million years ago
Great ice ages
First human beings – 0.35 million years ago

Yellow line: last 10,000 years of history

mon in interplanetary space. This atmosphere was probably short-lived because hydrogen atoms are too light to be retained very long by Earth's gravity, so they gradually leak off into space. (Jupiter is made almost entirely of hydrogen because it has enough gravity to prevent the gas from escaping.) Whatever Earth's original atmosphere was, the giant impact that created the Moon probably destroyed it. In fact, some scientists have speculated that after that unbelievably huge impact, for a very short time Earth may have had an atmosphere of hot, vaporized metal!

Meanwhile, volcanoes were pouring gases such as carbon dioxide (CO_2) and water vapor into the sky in vast quantities. Even today, water vapor forms 60 to 95 percent of the gases emitted by volcanoes. The volcanic gases of 4 to 4.5 billion years ago may have been even richer in water vapor. Because of the presence of such large quantities of heavy gases—that is, gases heavier than hydrogen—this early atmosphere may have been very dense, perhaps as much as 70 times as dense as it is today. This is similar to the present-day atmosphere of Venus, which is almost totally made up of carbon dioxide. It has a surface pressure 90 times that of Earth's—the equivalent of being under 3,000 feet (914 m) of water!

The First Ocean

As long as the crust remained hot, water condensing from the atmosphere simply boiled away again as steam. But as the crust cooled, liquid water began to collect in pools and lakes. Torrential rains poured from the cooling clouds, and soon the low-lying surface was covered in a worldwide ocean. The landscape of Earth

Facing page: The first oceans are formed as torrential rains pour from the sky.

4.4 billion years ago would have seemed like an alien planet from a science-fiction movie. The air would be thick and humid, the pressure crushing, and the temperature near boiling. The sky would be dark because of the high-altitude layer of dust. An endless ocean would stretch toward the horizon in every direction, broken only by volcanic islands and the curving rims of flooded craters.

But as the water vapor continued to fall as rain, the air pressure also decreased. The heavy carbon dioxide was absorbed by the new oceans, and this also brought about drops in the air pressure. The sky began to brighten some 4.2 billion years ago even though asteroids still fell, blasting huge craters in the landscape. The asteroid impacts also helped to thin the atmosphere as they blew some of it away into space. There were no long-lived surface features. Whatever land managed to rise above the waves was pounded by meteors or was worn away by the huge **tides** created by the nearby Moon, which was still much closer to Earth than it is today. When an asteroid impacted in the ocean, gigantic waves—**tsunamis**—miles high swept around the world, crumbling newly formed islands back into the sea. Some of these impacts may have been violent enough to have completely boiled away Earth's ocean, which eventually fell back as rain and re-formed.

The First Continents

Meanwhile, the first continents began to form. These may have been created by giant asteroid impacts. At the same time asteroids were blasting huge craters in the surface, the impacts were also

Facing page: Asteroids pummel the barren landscape of Earth's first continents.

piling up enormous masses of material. Since the asteroids fell randomly, more material eventually accumulated in some places than in others. Astronomer William K. Hartmann believes that the creation of just two vast craters might have built up enough debris between them to have formed a large, permanent landmass well above sea level.

Eventually—about 3.8 billion years ago—large asteroid impacts grew fewer until they were not much more frequent than they are today. The Moon receded to about 70 percent of the distance it is today, and Earth's rotation slowed to thirteen-and-a-half hours. The atmosphere was still mostly carbon dioxide. Still, even after such a violent birth filled with extraordinary events, a more remarkable one was yet to come.

CHAPTER FIVE

THE BIRTH OF LIFE

Between 4.2 and 3.5 billion years ago, Earth took a breather. The last of the debris left over from the formation of the solar system had been swept up by collisions with Earth, the Moon, and other planets. Dry land was emerging from the worldwide ocean as water evaporated into the thinning atmosphere. Earth would not yet have looked at all familiar. Its barren landscape of cold black rock was surrounded by a broad ocean. This ocean was murky with silt eroded from the fledgling continents by the constant rain and enormous tides. The sky would have been hazy, and the Sun would have rushed through it nearly twice as fast as it does now. When night fell, an enormous Moon nearly a third larger than the one we see today would rise into the cloudy sky.

Things might have seemed to be relatively quiet, but in fact the most extraordinary event to have occurred in the solar system was taking place. The vast, worldwide ocean was a soup of minerals and elements washed from the continents by rain, tides, and meteor impacts. The water also had vast amounts of carbon dioxide dissolved in it. These oceans, combined with the energy of sunlight, lightning, and tides, were the ingredients required for the beginning of life.

Carbon—which, along with oxygen, is one of the elements that form carbon dioxide (CO_2) in the oceans and atmosphere—has many special properties. Among them is the ability to form large, complex molecules in combination with a great many other elements, such as hydrogen, nitrogen, and oxygen. Another and perhaps even more important property of many carbon-based molecules is their ability to split into two identical halves. When they do this they reproduce themselves. This ability to reproduce is the foundation of life.

Billions of complex, self-reproducing molecules formed in the carbon-rich chemical soup of the early oceans. According to the most generally accepted theory, all that was needed to start the process of creating these molecules was a source of energy, and there were plenty of those: Ultraviolet light from the Sun, lightning, and the action of the tides were just some of the sources available. Billions of different complex molecules were the building blocks from which more complex life-forms developed.

No one knows when the first living cells evolved from these early, reproducing molecules. We do know that by at least 3.5 billion years ago there were true cells on Earth. Scientists have found their fossils in some of the oldest rocks on our planet, such as the 3.2-billion-year-old rocks found in South Africa and the 2-billion-year-old rocks of central Canada. These regions are the oldest remaining examples of Earth's original surface. It is very difficult to find such early evidences of life because there are few areas on Earth that have not been affected by geologic change over enormous periods of time. These geologic changes include asteroid

Facing page: As Earth's atmosphere finally clears, the Moon becomes visible. It is huge since it is much closer to Earth than it is today.

impacts, lava flows, mountain building, deposits of sediment from ancient oceans, and erosion by **weather**.

The First Living Things

The first simple life-forms to inhabit Earth were bacteria and their relatives, the blue-green algae. Both are still with us today, making them the oldest and most successful life-forms on our planet.

Between 2 and 3 billion years ago, a new type of cell came into being. Unlike the cells of bacteria or blue-green algae, these new cells possessed a **nucleus**, a tiny clump in their middle like the pit of a peach. The new cell's **DNA** was concentrated in the nucleus, where it was protected by a membrane. Before this, DNA was scattered throughout a cell, where it was subject to damage. Concentrating DNA made it easier for the cell to reproduce. Two types of these improved cells eventually evolved. One type resembled the original algae and was the ancestor of today's plants. The other, more complex version, called **protozoa**, evolved into animals.

A Change of Atmosphere

Until 2 to 3 billion years ago, the atmosphere of Earth was mostly carbon dioxide and water vapor. But by 2 to 2.3 billion years ago, life had become so abundant that it started to affect the environment. Like the process of photosynthesis in today's plants, blue-green algae used sunlight to break down atmospheric carbon

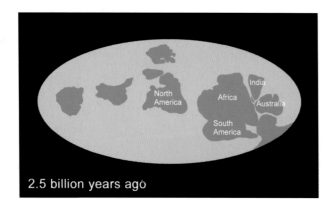

2.5 billion years ago

dioxide in order to obtain the carbon it needed to build organic molecules. The excess oxygen, which the algae didn't need, was released into the atmosphere (carbon dioxide [CO_2] is composed of one carbon atom and two oxygen atoms, so for every carbon atom the plant used two oxygen atoms were released). Eventually, through the efforts of countless trillions of these tiny organisms, most of the carbon dioxide in Earth's atmosphere was gradually replaced by oxygen.

Oxygen is a highly reactive gas that would not last long in the atmosphere if there weren't some way to constantly replace it. Normally, oxygen would rapidly combine with any iron in the soil to form rust, or with hydrogen to form water. The fact that there is any oxygen in our atmosphere at all is due entirely to the effects of Earth's plant life. It took many millions of years to create enough oxygen to raise it to today's level, where it accounts for about 21 percent of Earth's atmosphere. Two billion years ago, the proportion of oxygen was only about 1 percent.

It is just as well for the development of life that it took so long for large amounts of oxygen to accumulate because—amazingly enough—oxygen is actually dangerous to life-forms. It is such a reactive gas—meaning that it combines with other elements so rapidly that it can cause combustion—that life had to evolve special means to handle it. If some blue-green algae were to be transported from the ancient Earth to today's world, it would be quickly poisoned by the huge amounts of oxygen in our atmosphere. Even today's colonies of blue-green algae thrive best in oxygen-poor environments. Our own bodies have built-in

Mats of floating algae were among the earliest life-forms on Earth.

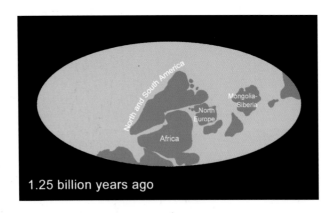

1.25 billion years ago

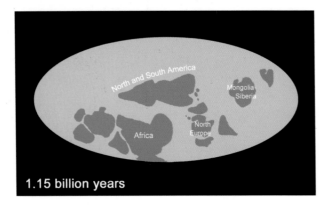

1.15 billion years

chemical protections against oxygen poisoning, inherited from our ancient one-celled ancestors.

Humans owe a lot to those primitive plants. Animal life requires a great deal of energy—much more than a plant, which stays in one place and lets the Sun provide all the energy it requires. An animal, however, searches for its own food, and to do so it must move around. This requires a constant source of high-quality energy. Animals obtain this by burning fuel. Burning means combining fuel with oxygen, which releases large amounts of energy in the process. (When a match burns, the heat comes from the combination of oxygen with the wood or paper in a process called **oxidation**. The warmth of your body comes from the heat produced by the oxidation of the food you eat.) Without a source of oxygen, animals would have had no way of quickly obtaining energy from their food. So the plants that laboriously filled Earth's atmosphere with oxygen made the **evolution** of animal life—and eventually human beings—possible.

CHAPTER SIX

THE FIRST ANIMALS

By 1 billion years ago the oxygen content of Earth's atmosphere was about the same as that we breathe today, but there was little else that would have seemed familiar. A map of the world would have looked very strange: We wouldn't recognize any of the continents, mountain ranges, or seas. Most of the landmasses were huddled around the equator or in the Southern Hemisphere. Even though life was abundant, it would not have been apparent. Life had not yet made the transition to dry land.

Occasionally, vast sheets of ice crept down from the poles, using up so much of Earth's water that the sea level lowered. The first **ice age** we know of occurred 2.3 billion years ago. It may have lasted as long as a hundred million years. But the Sun was then beginning to grow warmer, so the ice eventually retreated. There is evidence of several other ice ages between 900 and 600 million years ago, a period that some scientists refer to as "the longest winter."

An Explosion of Life

By 700 million years ago, there were distinctive forms of plant and animal life in the seas. Over the next 150 million years there was virtually an explosion of life-forms of all kinds. Life quickly evolved from primitive one-celled plants and animals to complex multi-celled organisms with muscles, organs, and nerves. By 550 million years ago, hard-shelled creatures developed, such as the **brachiopod**, a kind of clam, and the **trilobite**, a distant ancestor of the horseshoe crab. Life flourished so abundantly that fossils from this period are found on every continent.

Why did life suddenly proliferate, and make so much progress, in such a short time? No one knows for certain, though there are several theories that try to account for it. One suggests that it was due to the ordinary forces of evolution, though evolution would seem to be too slow a process for such rapid changes to occur. Another theory holds that the development of **sexual reproduction** is responsible. Sexual reproduction, as opposed to **asexual**, or single-parent, reproduction, would have allowed the rapid, efficient mixing of genes that encouraged useful **mutations** to spread quickly. Other theories suggest that the proliferation of life was due to environmental changes, such as the increase in oxygen content or the warmer seas following the first great ice age. The answer may lie in one of these theories, or, more likely, a combination of several.

By 450 million years ago, the first fish were swimming in Earth's seas. These were primitive, jawless creatures that cruised the ocean floors looking for food. Fifty million years later, those harmless creatures had evolved into fearsome monsters, sharklike carnivores 30 feet (9 m) long preying on other fish that had developed armor plating for protection.

Finally, between 450 and 400 million years ago, life finally braved the move to dry land. At first only mosses and lichens grew on the barren rocks, but by the end of this period the continents were covered with forests of ferns and other primitive, seedless plants.

The first life-forms to exist on dry land were probably mosses and lichens, which are shown here as greenish patches near the edge of the water.

Evolution is both a fact and a theory. No scientist doubts that evolution occurs; what is debated is just how evolution works. Charles Darwin laid the basic groundwork in 1859 when he published *On the Origin of Species*. Since then, however, his theory has been greatly revised and expanded upon. One group of scientists thinks that it works steadily and slowly, while another group thinks it works in sudden fits and starts, with bursts of biological changes occurring between periods of relative inactivity.

In spite of the disagreement over details, the fundamental idea behind evolution has remained fairly solid since Darwin. He held that useful qualities are passed down from generation to generation while harmful ones die out. For instance, an animal whose neck is slightly longer than its fellows may have an advantage in obtaining food. Therefore, it has a better chance at survival and passing its genes on to later generations, which will also have the advantage of the longer neck. Creatures with less useful characteristics have a reduced chance of surviving and passing on their genes. In this way, over long periods of time, changes are gradually made in animals and plants.

CHAPTER SEVEN

EARTH TAKES SHAPE

Meanwhile, as the shape of life was changing, Earth was undergoing its own evolution. Earth's crust is not one solid, unbroken layer of rock. It is formed of separate chunks, called **plates**. Each plate can be thought of as a kind of raft floating on top of the semi-molten mantle beneath, like ice on a pond. Some of these plates carry the continents. Since the hot mantle is semi-fluid, currents circulate through it. If you've ever noticed how oatmeal churns in a pan as it's cooking, you've seen exactly how currents circulate in the hot mantle. Like rafts carried by ocean currents, the plates of Earth are moved around by the currents in the mantle. Sometimes these currents cause plates to split and pull apart; other times plates will collide with one another.

You can envision what occurs if you lay two sheets of paper on a tabletop and push them together, edge-to-edge. One sheet might be shoved over the top of another, or the sheets might buckle and crumple where they meet. The same things happen when plates collide. One might be shoved beneath another one. When this happens, the lower plate is melted when it reaches the hot mantle. Or the plates might crumple like colliding cars. This forms mountain ranges. Two side-by-side plates may move in opposite directions. For instance, one plate may be moving north

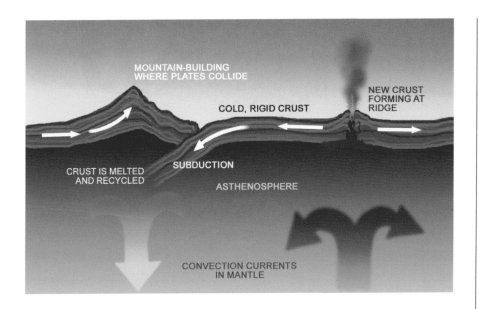

MOUNTAIN-BUILDING
WHERE PLATES COLLIDE

NEW CRUST
FORMING AT
RIDGE

COLD, RIGID CRUST

CRUST IS MELTED
AND RECYCLED

SUBDUCTION

ASTHENOSPHERE

CONVECTION CURRENTS
IN MANTLE

Plate tectonics: As the semi-molten material deep beneath Earth's crust circulates, it carries the hard, outer crust with it. Where material rises from beneath, the crust spreads apart and cracks, and fresh crust is created. Where material sinks, crustal plates collide and create mountains.

and another south. If you press the palm of your hand on a table-top and then try to slide it, it won't move smoothly. Instead it'll move in jerks and leaps. The same thing occurs when plates try to move past one another. They "stick" and move in sudden jerks and leaps, which creates earthquakes.

When plates pull apart, fresh lava wells up from beneath, creating new continental rocks. This is happening right now in many places on Earth. The Atlantic Ocean is a huge split between the plates that carry North and South America and the plates that carry Europe and Africa. Running down the middle of the Atlantic is a crack called the Midatlantic Ridge, where fresh material is constantly rising to the surface. This is the newest land on Earth.

As the plates slowly drift around the surface of Earth, the continents are carried along with them. This means that the appearance of Earth has changed a great deal over millions of years . . . and is still changing, for that matter, as Earth's plates move at a rate of about 0.8–4 inches (2–10 cm) a year.

An Alien Earth

If we could see Earth as it looked 500 million years ago we would not recognize it. There were only two large continental masses, which scientists call Laurasia and Gondwanaland. Between them was a narrow belt of water called the Tethyan Seaway. The rest of the world was covered by ocean. After 300 million years had passed, these continents crowded together into one supercontinent, called Pangaea, with the Tethyan Sea squeezed into a series of narrow lakes. The formation of Gondwanaland was a boon for the development of life on Earth. Since it was one huge landmass straddling the equator, the climate was warm with few seasonal changes. This was perfect for the rapid evolution of life.

But the plates are always moving, and the continents, which must move with them, are always changing. The Tethyan Sea grew wide again as Laurasia split from Gondwanaland. The plates that carried them also began to split, separating Laurasia and Gondwanaland into even smaller continents. Laurasia broke up into what was to become North America and Eurasia, while Gondwanaland split into the future Africa, South America, Antarctica, and India. By 100 million years ago, the rough shapes of today's continents began to take form.

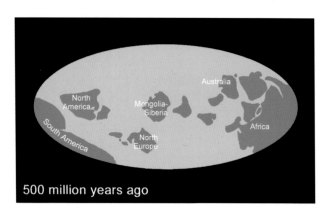

500 million years ago

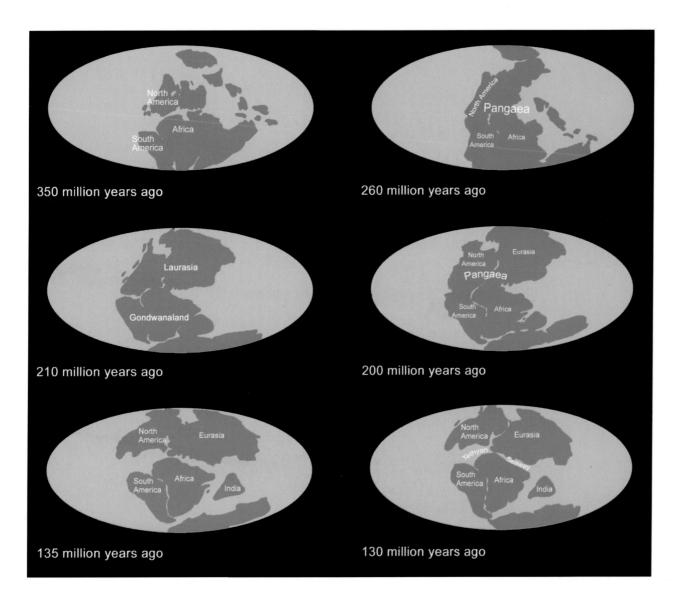

350 million years ago

260 million years ago

210 million years ago

200 million years ago

135 million years ago

130 million years ago

CHAPTER EIGHT

THE RISE AND FALL OF THE DINOSAURS

Life swept over the continents like a tidal wave. By 320 million years ago, great forests covered the world. Spiders, scorpions, millipedes, cockroaches, and foot-long dragonflies shared the land with the ancestors of today's frogs and salamanders, which in turn had evolved from lobe-finned lungfish. These first amphibians were the predecessors of the reptiles that came to dominate Earth for tens of millions of years.

The Great Extinction

About 250 million years ago a mysterious catastrophe nearly wiped all life from our planet. As much as 90 percent of all species died out. The trilobites disappeared, as did most of the clamlike animals. Three of the four orders of amphibians vanished. Of the fifty genera of mammal-like reptiles, only one survived. It was this one genus from which all modern mammals—including human beings—evolved. We came awfully close to not being here at all.

All of this occurred within a few million years, in a period called the Great Extinction. No one is at all certain exactly what caused this disaster. Theories range from glacial cooling and global warming to radiation from a nearby **supernova** or perhaps even an impact by an asteroid or comet.

So many species disappeared at the end of the Great Extinction that the way was opened for some of the surviving species, who now had much less competition, to proliferate wildly. The reptiles were among these. From 250 million years ago to 65 million years ago—a span of 185 million years—they dominated the world. It was the age of the dinosaurs. Although many people think of dinosaurs as having been an evolutionary failure, since they are all long extinct, they were actually far more successful than humans, who have only been on Earth for fewer than 4 million years (if we generously include our most distant humanlike ancestors). The dinosaurs existed fifty times longer than that.

The Age of Reptiles

Dinosaurs spread all over Earth. Their fossils have been found on every continent. During the 185 million years they existed, dinosaurs and other reptiles evolved into hundreds of different varieties. There were the ferocious, carnivorous monsters that are so familiar to today's moviegoers—the tyrannosaurs, the velociraptors—and enormous, plodding planteaters such as the brontosaurus and stegosaurus. They ranged in size from the 140-foot (43-m)-long seismosaurus to creatures hardly larger than a chicken. They took to the sea, filling the oceans with sea-serpentlike plesiosaurs and killer-whalelike ichthyosaurs. They even took to the air. The pterodactyl glided on leathery, batlike wings that spanned as much as 6 feet (1.8 m) from tip to tip, while the giant ptero-

The first dinosaurs appeared over 250 million years ago and flourished for more than 185 million years until they mysteriously died out.

dactyloid had a wingspan of 39 feet (12 m), the size of a small airplane.

But even the fabulous reign of the dinosaurs came to an end, and it did so in a fashion as big and spectacular as the dinosaurs themselves. According to the most generally accepted theory, the end was caused by a rock 6 miles (10 km) wide. It was nothing compared to the asteroid that created the Moon, which may have been a thousand times larger, but it was more than enough to wipe nearly all life from our planet.

The End of the Dinosaurs

The asteroid hit in the region of present-day Yucatán, Mexico. It was probably traveling at a speed of at least 10 miles (16 km) per second. It struck Earth with the force of 100 million one-megaton hydrogen bombs. (Each megaton is equivalent to a million tons of TNT, a high explosive.) The asteroid and the ground beneath it were instantly transformed into a titanic explosion of vaporized rock and steam that expanded at the speed of sound. A crater nearly 125 miles (200 km) wide was formed. A vast plume of debris sprayed high into the atmosphere. The impact created earthquakes of unprecedented violence. If the asteroid had hit in the shallow sea off the Yucatán coast, a tsunami wave up to 3 miles (5 km) high would have devastated nearby low-lying lands. Even distant shores would have been impacted by waves thousands of feet high.

It was not the devastating violence of the impact that spelled the end for so many species, but the aftermath. Within an hour of the explosion, millions of tons of red-hot debris began to fall back

Facing page: The age of the dinosaurs might have been brought to an end by the aftereffects of an asteroid impact with Earth.

(42)

Within a few minutes of the asteroid's impact, ash began to fall, continuing for up to six months or more. Sunlight was blocked, and plant and animal life began to die out on the dark, cold Earth.

onto Earth, a rain of fire that ignited forests all over the world. A forest fire would have raged over the planet for months, destroying life and habitats and pouring vast clouds of smoke into the sky.

Rain would have fallen in a deluge, but even the rain would have been deadly. The shock of the explosion would have converted much of the nitrogen and oxygen in Earth's atmosphere into nitrogen oxides, a major ingredient of acid rain. This would have been at a much higher concentration than the acid rain that is so dangerous to today's forests and animal life. Some scientists believe that it might have been the main cause for the great extinction following the impact.

Meanwhile, the vast amount of dust that had been thrown into the upper atmosphere—abetted by the smoke and ash from the global forest fire—began to blanket Earth. The Sun grew dim, and Earth began to grow cold. For several months, the world was plunged into total darkness, and for months after that it was as dim as a moonlit night. Without sunlight, plants (and the plankton that lived in the oceans that were the basis of its food chain) could not photosynthesize food and died. And without plants and plankton to eat, animals died. Seventy-five percent of all the species on Earth did not survive long after the impact.

CHAPTER NINE

EARTH TODAY

It might seem strange to title this chapter "Earth Today," since there were still 65 million years between the time of the asteroid impact that caused the extinction of the dinosaurs and the twenty-first century. But that 65-million-year period is only 1 percent of the entire history of our planet. If all the time that has passed since the formation of Earth were to be compressed into a calendar in which each day was equal to 100 million years, then Earth would only be about 46 days old. Life did not come about until 10 days ago. The dinosaurs did not begin their reign until yesterday and the impact that wiped them out occurred at 8:00 this morning. The first humans did not walk the planet until about 15 minutes before midnight, and the first landing on the Moon occurred in the last one-hundredth second of today.

If we were to visit the Earth of 60 million years ago, it would seem very familiar. The continents had much the same shape that they do today. The Atlantic Ocean would seem oddly narrow, since it was still widening as North and South America receded from Europe and Africa. Meanwhile, Australia had broken away from Antarctica. It moved northward, while the latter headed toward the South Pole. A small section of eastern Africa had also

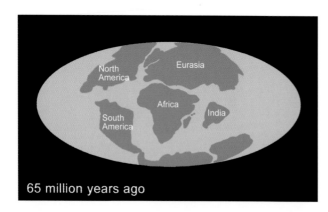

65 million years ago

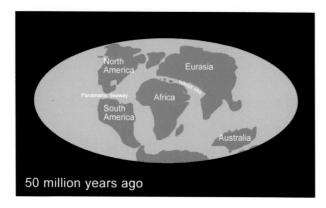

50 million years ago

broken away. It was moving across the Indian Ocean and would soon run into Asia, creating present-day India. The collision created the Himalayan Mountains. Many other mountain ranges that are familiar to us today, such as the Rockies, were created 60 to 65 million years ago. The Rockies of North America and the Andes of South America grew along the leading edges of the continents as they plowed into the Pacific Ocean, like dirt in front of a bulldozer.

Meanwhile, the survivors of the asteroid impact were evolving into new kinds of animals. Without the competition of the giant lizards, tiny mammals began to flourish, and within 10 million years the first **primates**—our distant ancestors—appeared. These were mouse-sized, omnivorous tree-dwellers similar to today's tarsiers and lemurs. Unlike the highly specialized creatures that had preceded them, these new animals had all-purpose survival skills. Also, they were able and willing to eat just about anything.

The Rise of Humankind

About 35 million years ago, some of these early primates evolved into the first true monkeys and apes. Three groups of primates developed independently—one in South America, one in Asia, and one in Africa. Only five examples of the third group survive to this day: gibbons, orangutans, gorillas, chimpanzees, and humans. The first humans seem to have appeared in Africa 4 or 5 million years ago. They are called **australopithecines** and were probably chimpanzeelike creatures that stood only about 4 to 5 feet (1.2 to 1.5 m) tall. They were ground-dwellers and walked upright. Although their brains were only about half the size of a modern human's, by 2.5 million years ago they were using tools made of bone and stone.

As humanlike creatures evolved, they spread from Africa into Europe and Asia. **Homo sapiens**, or "wise man," evolved about 350,000 years ago. In fact, there were two varieties of Homo sapiens: the **Neanderthals** and the **Cro-Magnons**. The Neanderthals thrived until just 35,000 years ago but mysteriously died out. The Cro-Magnons roamed Africa 50,000 years ago and soon spread through Europe, Asia, and, eventually, North and South America. They fought many wars between their tribes, built great cities, established vast empires, and fought more wars. As the centuries and millennia passed, they wrote books, created religions and invented science, built machines and palaces and places of worship, and traveled to the Moon. How long will this upstart species last? It's too soon to tell.

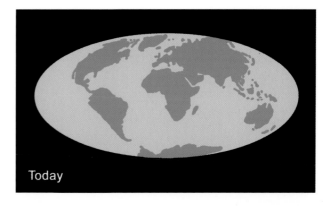

Today

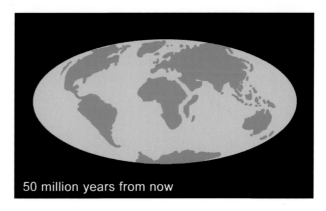

50 million years from now

Earth is still changing. If the continents continue to drift as they have in the past, Earth will look very different in the future. Among the changes that may occur 50 million years from now, Africa will separate from Eurasia and split in two, India will move farther north, and the west coast of America will drift into the Pacific Ocean.

CHAPTER TEN

EARTH AROUND US

The Earth we see around us is a diverse collection of landscapes: deserts, ice caps, mountains, valleys, glaciers, rain forests, volcanoes, oceans, and prairies. Even from day to day, the world can seem different as the weather changes and the seasons go through their yearly cycles. The shape of the landscape outside your window is mainly a product of these forces: mountains and hills built up by colliding plates and eroded by wind and water; valleys carved by rivers and streams; plains scoured by glaciers; and fields and forests of plant life.

Even though most geologic forces are far too slow to be perceived in an entire human lifetime—except when something drastic happens, such as an earthquake—things such as weather and the daily movement of Earth are not only visible, they are vital to our lives and well-being. Predicting the annual change of seasons was important for the development of agriculture. Taking advantage of Earth's magnetic field by the use of compasses helped humans explore their planet. Understanding the workings of weather has saved trillions of dollars and millions of lives.

The Moon, 240,000 miles (386,000 km) away, rises above Earth in this photograph taken by an Apollo astronaut. Earth's atmosphere lies in the hazy blue blanket below. The airless sky above is black. [NASA]

The Sahara Desert (left) and the Gulf Coast of Texas and the Gulf of Mexico (right) are examples of the diverse collection of landscapes that scatter Earth. [NASA]

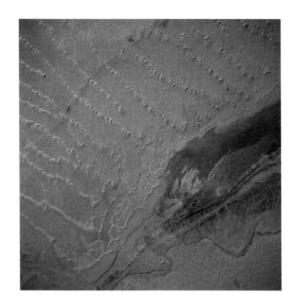

Weather

The Sun is the ultimate source of power that drives Earth's weather. It warms its surface and the oceans, and it evaporates water from rivers, lakes, and seas. The tropical regions—the areas directly to the north and south of the equator—are heated more than the poles because the sunlight shines more directly on the tropics. Because of this uneven heating, the atmosphere swirls like water boiling in a pan, with warm air rising and cool air rushing in to fill the space.

If Earth did not rotate, the currents of air would flow smoothly from the tropics to the poles. But Earth does rotate. (At the equator it spins at 1,000 miles per hour [1,609 km/h], with

The Nile River delta and the eastern Mediterranean Sea seen from an orbiting spacecraft (the dark triangle in the lower right corner is part of the spacecraft window): Only the area around the river is cultivated—the rest is desert. Knowing when the Nile would flood was important to the ancient Egyptians. This led to the creation of the first calendars. [NASA]

A hurricane seen from space: The spiral shape is created by the spinning of Earth. [NASA]

the speed diminishing toward the poles.) This causes the currents of air to swerve to one side, so that winds tend to move in spirals instead of straight lines. Sometimes these spirals, powered by warm ocean waters, tighten into whirling circular storms, or hurricanes. As these large air currents pass over continents, oceans, mountains, plains, and deserts, the patterns of weather become more complicated, so weather changes from day to day and from season to season. Some of these effects are very subtle and some are large-scale, but they all play a role in creating our daily weather.

As the Sun warms lakes, oceans, and rivers, the water in them evaporates and rises into the atmosphere. On a clear day this water vapor is invisible. We are aware of its presence only when it forms clouds or falls as rain or snow. Earth's winds help to distribute water vapor from areas with a great deal of water, such as forests and grasslands, to areas with little water, such as deserts.

Weather and **climate** are often confused. Weather refers to the changes from day to day or week to week, while climate refers to the average of a large area over a long period of time. A region with a dry climate, such as a desert, can still have rainy days, just as Hawaii, which has a rainy climate, can have sunny, dry days. The climate of Earth has been gradually growing warmer, because it is still slowly emerging from the last ice age, which ended only 10,000 years ago. Gases—such as CO_2—created by burning **fossil fuels** are making this warming happen more quickly.

The Air Around Us

We live at the bottom of an ocean of air more than 60 miles (100 km) deep. The atmosphere really has no "top"—it just grows thinner and thinner until it merges with the vacuum of space. However, above 60 miles (100 km) there is so little air that it is usually considered to be where space starts.

A column of air one square inch reaching from the surface of Earth to the top of the atmosphere weighs 15 pounds (6.8 kg). This is called **atmospheric pressure**. There are 15 pounds (6.8 kg) of air pressing on every square inch of your body (which means that your entire body might be supporting as much as

The effect of the spinning Earth on the moving air currents is called the **Coriolis effect**. This effect causes air currents traveling between the poles and the equator to move in curves. A playground carousel demonstrates how this happens. Two children are riding on it on opposite sides. While the carousel is standing still, one tosses a ball to her friend (A). He will have no trouble catching it since it travels straight toward him. Then the carousel starts spinning. While it is turning, she tosses the ball to her friend again. Instead of traveling directly toward him, it curves away to one side (B). In exactly the same way, the Coriolis effect causes the winds on Earth to curve to one side or the other as they move between the equator and the poles. It is the Coriolis effect that makes storms such as hurricanes spin in huge circles.

In the case of an airless world, such as Mercury or the Moon, the heat received at the surface from the Sun is radiated back out into space. But if the planet has an atmosphere, as Earth does, the situation changes. An atmosphere traps much of the incoming solar radiation, keeping it from radiating back out into space, so the temperature at the surface can become very hot. This kind of heating is called a **greenhouse effect**.

The glass panes of a greenhouse allow the infrared radiation of sunlight to penetrate, but prevent the heat from escaping. This is because the infrared radiation from the Sun is much more energetic, or powerful, than the heat radiated by

Powerful infrared radiation from the Sun penetrates Earth's atmosphere and heats the surface.

Infrared radiation from the surface is too weak to penetrate the atmosphere.

Since more heat comes in than escapes, the surface gets hotter and hotter.

warm soil. This lower-energy heat cannot escape back out through the glass. The temperature inside the greenhouse becomes greater than the temperature outside.

The carbon dioxide (and to some extent the water vapor) in Earth's atmosphere acts like the glass panes in a greenhouse: It allows the high-energy infrared radiation from the Sun to pass through but prevents the low-energy infrared radiation from the surface from escaping back into space. Fortunately for us, there is not enough CO_2 in our atmosphere to keep in all of the heat, and most of it does manage to escape. It's as though there are some panes missing in the roof of the greenhouse. The atmosphere of the early Earth, however, was almost entirely CO_2, so most of the heat the planet received from the Sun was trapped beneath the clouds, unable to escape.

20,000 pounds [9,072 kg]!). The pressure grows less the higher you rise above the ground because there is less air above you. If you have ever felt your ears pop as you rose in an elevator or airplane, you have experienced the effect of changing air pressure.

The lowest part of the atmosphere, from ground level to about 6 miles (10 km), is called the **troposphere**. All of Earth's weather takes place within the troposphere. Extending above the troposphere to about 30 miles (48 km) is the **stratosphere**. Most of the oxygen in the stratosphere is in the form of **ozone**. The oxygen we breathe is in the form of a molecule consisting of two atoms (O_2). Ozone consists of three atoms (O_3). Ozone is very good at filtering dangerous ultraviolet radiation from sunlight. Life on Earth would be endangered if the ozone layer were to disappear.

Above the ozone layer is the **mesosphere**, which rises to about 50 miles (80 km). The uppermost layer is the **thermosphere**, which eventually merges with outer space.

Earth as a Magnet

As the molten iron core of Earth slowly churns, it generates a powerful magnetic field in much the same way that the generator in a power plant creates an electric current. This magnetic field is easily detected—in fact, it was detected long before anyone even knew what magnetism was. Thousands of years ago, the Chinese discovered that if a needle was rubbed against a lodestone (an iron ore that is a natural magnet) and then hung from a thread or floated in water on a cork, it would always

(55)

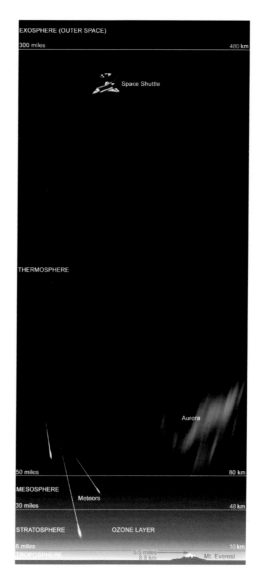

EXOSPHERE (OUTER SPACE)
300 miles · 480 km
Space Shuttle
THERMOSPHERE
Aurora
50 miles · 80 km
MESOSPHERE
Meteors
30 miles · 48 km
STRATOSPHERE · OZONE LAYER
6 miles · 10 km
TROPOSPHERE · 5.5 miles / 8.8 km · Mt. Everest

A cross section of Earth's atmosphere

The auroras are caused by particles from the Sun interacting with gases high in Earth's atmosphere, causing them to glow.

point in the same direction. The compass was developed to take advantage of this phenomenon and was quickly adapted for use by navigators on ships.

A good way to imagine the magnetic field of Earth is to think of a rubber ball with a bar magnet stuck through its middle. A compass placed anywhere on the surface of the ball will point toward the North Pole of the magnet. When you use a compass you are detecting the natural magnetic field of Earth.

The magnetic field is very important to life on Earth. It shields our planet from the dangerous particles emitted by the Sun. These flow toward Earth in a constant stream called the **solar wind**. Some of these particles would be very dangerous if they reached the ground, but our magnetic field causes most of them to swerve harmlessly around Earth. Other particles carried along by the magnetic field spiral in toward the North and South Poles of the planet. When these high-energy particles hit the upper atmosphere, they cause the molecules of gas there to glow in much the same way that the electricity flowing through a neon tube causes the gas inside it to glow. The glowing gases in the upper atmosphere are often visible from the surface as shimmering bands and curtains of colored light. These are called the **auroras**.

CHAPTER ELEVEN

A PLANET ON THE MOVE

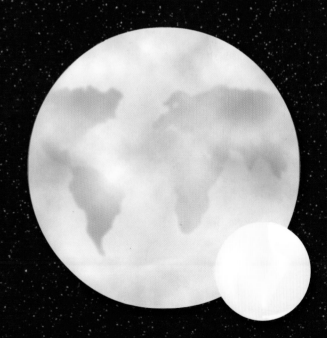

The motions of Earth and the Moon were known and used by human beings long before anyone realized that Earth was a planet or the Moon a world. The regular succession of night and day was probably the first measure of time used by humans. The phases of the Moon were probably the next most noticeable event; and time was divided into days and months long before it was divided into seasons and years.

Earth has probably always been the same distance from the Sun, so the length of the year has been pretty much unchanged since the planet formed, but the length of the day has changed drastically over billions of years. Shortly after the Moon was created, the length of the day was only about five hours. It has been gradually increasing ever since, mainly due to the drag exerted on Earth by the tides, which are caused by the Moon.

A Few Facts

Earth is a huge ball of rock and metal spinning through space at an incredible speed. It is 7,927 miles (12,756 km) in diameter. Its

The Moon is the easiest to observe of all our neighbors in space. Its phases can easily be seen with the naked eye, and even a small telescope or pair of binoculars will reveal amazing details, such as craters and mountains. With a good map, you can find your way around the surface as easily as you might find your way around the neighborhood in which you live. Observe the Moon over a period of time, and see how the changing angle of sunlight makes the surface look different.

There are so many ways in which to observe Earth that they have become separate sciences in their own right, such as geology, geography, meteorology, and oceanography. Almost all of these can be enjoyed by a student or an amateur scientist. For instance, you could begin a collection of rocks and minerals or you could start a weather diary. A number of good books and Web sites that can get you started are listed at the end of this book.

The Moon as it looks through a pair of ordinary binoculars

surface has an area of 197,359,949 square miles (511,160,000 sq km). Of this, approximately only 50,000,000 square miles (129,500,000 sq km) are land—the remaining three quarters is covered by water. It circles the Sun at an average distance of 93,000,000 miles (149,637,000 km).

Earth traces a vast circle—its orbit—approximately 584,000,000 miles (939,656,000 km) in circumference around the Sun. The time it takes Earth to do this once is considered a year. Every day Earth must travel 1,600,000 miles (2,574,400 km) at a speed of 66,667 miles an hour (107,290 km/h). Every hour, Earth travels a distance equal to more than eight times its own diameter.

The Moving Earth

As Earth circles the Sun, it is spinning on its axis, like a top. The time it takes to spin around once is considered a day. The circumference (or equator) of Earth is 24,900 miles (40,070 km). This means that at the equator Earth is spinning at a speed of 24,900 miles per day, or 1,037 miles an hour (1,669 km/h). You don't notice the speed of Earth's rotation because you and everything else on the planet are being carried along with it. The same thing happens when you are traveling in car, train, or airplane. An airliner might be moving hundreds of miles an hour, but you can walk around inside as easily as if the plane were standing still. For the same reason, you can walk around on Earth and not notice that it is rapidly spinning.

Day and night are caused by the rotation of Earth. As it turns, every place on its surface is first turned toward the Sun and then away from it. At noon, you are directly beneath the Sun. It is daylight. Twelve hours later, Earth has rotated and you are on the side of Earth opposite the Sun. You are in the midst of Earth's shadow. It is midnight, and it is dark.

If the axis of Earth were straight up and down, days and nights would always be of equal length. But the axis is tipped 23.45 degrees. (This tilt may have been caused by the impact that created the Moon. The body that hit Earth may have knocked it sideways.) This changes everything. Days are still 24 hours long, but the amount of daylight versus night changes during the course of a year. At the latitude of New York City, for instance, the period of daylight can be as long as fifteen hours and as short as nine. At the poles, the tilt of Earth brings days and nights as long as six months each.

In addition to changing the length of daylight, the tilt also creates the seasons. During most of the year, part of Earth is tipped toward the Sun and is getting more sunlight and warmth, and another part is tipped away and is getting less sunlight and warmth. When the Northern Hemisphere is tilted toward the Sun, the days are longer and the Sun is high in the sky. The weather is warmer, and we have summer. Six months later, the Northern Hemisphere is tilted away from the Sun; the days are shorter and the Sun is low in the sky. The temperature grows cold, and we have winter.

FAST FACTS ABOUT EARTH

DIAMETER (at the equator): 7,927 miles (12,756 km)

DISTANCE FROM THE SUN: 93,000,000 miles (149,637,000 km)

LENGTH OF DAY: 23.93 hours

LENGTH OF YEAR: 365.2 days

The seasons are created by the tilt of Earth's axis. It is winter in the hemisphere that is tilted away from the Sun. Not only are the days shorter, the Sun's rays hit the ground at an angle. This keeps them from warming the ground as well as they do in summer.

Needed: Flashlight

Winter is cold because sunlight reaches the ground at a much greater angle than it does during the summer. The same amount of light arrives, but it is spread over a larger area. Since it is spread thinner, it warms less. Hold a flashlight a few feet above a tabletop and shine the light directly down on it. See how bright the circle of light is? Now slowly tilt the flashlight so the light hits the tabletop at an angle. See what happens to the circle of light? It spreads out over a larger and larger area, and as it does so it becomes dimmer. Just as the light is weakened by arriving at an angle, so is the heat that comes with it.

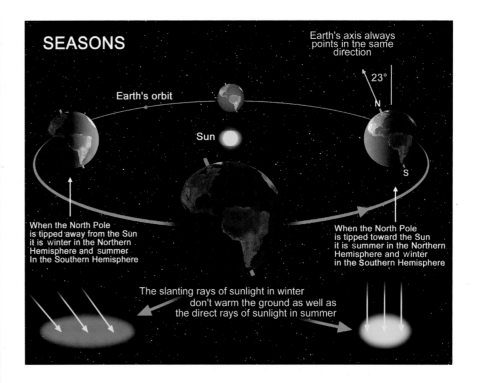

SEASONS

Earth's axis always points in the same direction

23°

Earth's orbit

Sun

When the North Pole is tipped away from the Sun it is winter in the Northern Hemisphere and summer in the Southern Hemisphere

When the North Pole is tipped toward the Sun it is summer in the Northern Hemisphere and winter in the Southern Hemisphere

The slanting rays of sunlight in winter don't warm the ground as well as the direct rays of sunlight in summer

Many people think that summer and winter are caused by the changing distance of Earth from the Sun—that it is closer in summer and farther away in winter. Actually, Earth is slightly closer to the Sun in January and farthest away in July. Seasons in the Southern Hemisphere are the opposite of those in the Northern. When it is winter in the United States it is summer in Australia, and vice versa.

CHAPTER TWELVE

A VISIT TO THE MOON

The Moon, one-quarter the size of our planet, orbits Earth in the same way that Earth orbits the Sun. It is 238,600 miles (384,000 km) away, circling Earth once every 27.3 days.

Other than collecting many craters, the Moon has changed very little in the 4 billion years since its creation. When our earliest ancestors looked up at the night sky, they saw essentially the same Moon you see today. It is certainly the most familiar of all our neighbors in space. The fact that the Moon always shows the same face to us leads a lot of people to assume that the Moon does not rotate. It does, of course. If it didn't, it wouldn't be able to always keep one side toward Earth. You can see for yourself why this is true. Put a chair in the middle of a room. Now walk around the chair while facing it the whole time. When you get back to where you started you will find that you will have also faced all four walls of the room. You could not have done this if you had not made one rotation on your axis while you made one **revolution** around the chair.

Another misconception about the Moon is that it has a permanent dark side. Many people talk about a "dark side of the

There are signs of ice in deep craters at the lunar poles. These areas are in permanent darkness—sunlight never reaches them.

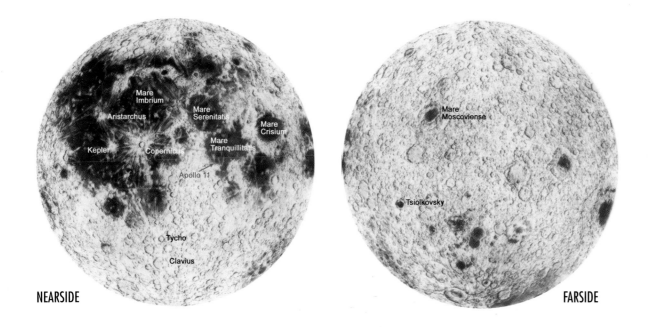

NEARSIDE

Mare Imbrium
Aristarchus
Mare Serenitatis
Mare Crisium
Kepler
Copernicus
Mare Tranquillitatis
Apollo 11
Tycho
Clavius

FARSIDE

Mare Moscoviense
Tsiolkovsky

Moon" that can never be seen from Earth. While it is true that the side of the Moon facing away from Earth—more properly called the **farside**—can never be seen from here, it is not always dark. As the Moon circles Earth, almost every part of its surface is eventually lit by the Sun. During the period known as the "new moon"—when the Moon is invisible in the night sky—the side facing us is dark, and the side facing away from Earth is sunlit.

As the Moon circles Earth, it does more than make our nights pleasant. It has a very direct, important effect on our planet. The Moon's gravity pulls on Earth as it circles it. Since the Moon is so close, it pulls more strongly on the side of Earth closest to it. (Earth does the same thing to the Moon, of course.) This uneven

Map of the lunar nearside (the side that always faces Earth) and farside (the side that always faces away from Earth). The farside does not have the large mare regions that distinguish the nearside. [NASA]

tug on our planet is called a **body tide**. The amount that the surface of Earth rises and falls as the Moon passes overhead is so small that it is hard to detect.

But the Moon does not pull on just the body of Earth; it also pulls on the oceans. The ocean tides are much easier to detect, since they can range from about 2 feet (0.6 m) to over 50 feet (15 m). This range in heights is due to factors such as the depth of the water and the shapes of coastlines. These also affect the time tides occur, though generally there are two high tides and two low tides every day. (The giant waves that are sometimes caused by earthquakes or volcanic eruptions are often called "tidal waves," though they have nothing to do with tides at all. The proper name for them is *tsunamis*.)

Tides are caused by the uneven gravitational attraction of the Moon on Earth. The side of Earth nearest the Moon is attracted more than the side farther away. This attraction raises the level of the oceans into a bulge. This bulge is carried around Earth as the Moon revolves in its orbit.

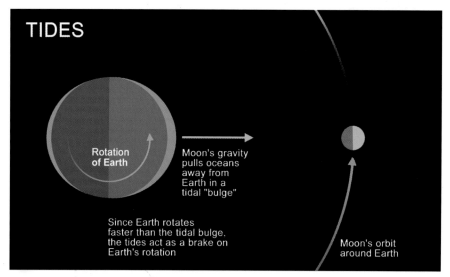

TIDES

Rotation of Earth

Moon's gravity pulls oceans away from Earth in a tidal "bulge"

Since Earth rotates faster than the tidal bulge, the tides act as a brake on Earth's rotation

Moon's orbit around Earth

From night to night, the Moon appears to change its shape. Sometimes it's a full, round disk, sometimes a thin crescent. These are called the Moon's **phases**. As the Moon circles Earth, the Sun lights the Moon from different angles. During a *full moon*, the Moon is on the opposite side of Earth from the Sun. Full moons rise as the Sun sets. During a *quarter moon*, the Moon, Earth, and the Sun are at right angles. A quarter moon will be overhead at sunset. (Many people call this a "half moon." Astronomers say "quarter moon" because they can see only one fourth of the entire surface of the Moon.) A *new moon* is between Earth and the Sun, so the dark side is facing us and we cannot see it. Between these phases are *crescent moons* and *gibbous moons*.

Seen from the Moon, Earth goes through phases, too. The phases of Earth are always exactly opposite those of the Moon. During a new moon, for instance, someone on the Moon would see a full Earth, and vice versa.

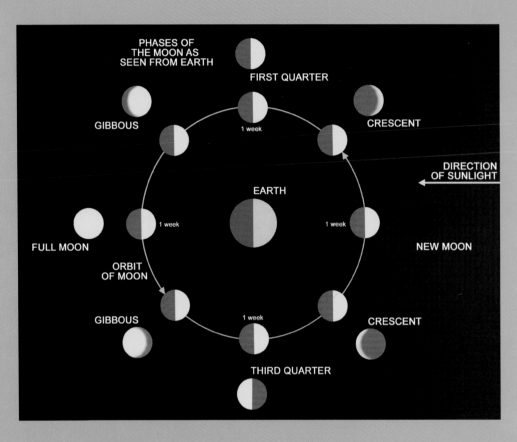

The phases of the Moon are caused by its changing relationship to the Sun.

The Apollo 11 mission landed the first humans on the Moon, July 20, 1969. [NASA]

THE APOLLO MISSIONS

Mission	Arrival date	Landing site	Accomplishments
Apollo 11	July 20, 1969	Mare Tranquillitatis	First lunar landing
Apollo 12	November 19, 1969	Oceanus Procellarum	Retrieved samples from the earlier, unmanned Surveyor landing
Apollo 14	February 5, 1971	Fra Mauro	Explored lunar highlands
Apollo 15	July 30, 1971	Hadley-Apennine	Explored lunar mountains and rills
Apollo 16	April 21, 1972	Descartes	Explored lunar mountains and other features
Apollo 17	December 11, 1972	Taurus-Littrow	Traveled farthest over lunar surface; returned the most samples

A rill, probably created by flowing lava [NASA]

Astronauts exploring Hadley Rille [NASA]

If Earth had not had a Moon, it is possible that we would not yet have flown into space. It was seeing another world high above us that inspired humans to want to travel away from Earth. After sending a few robotic probes to the Moon, human beings finally landed on the surface on July 20, 1969. The Apollo 11 mission carried three men to the Moon, Michael Collins, Neil Armstrong, and Edwin "Buzz" Aldrin. Collins remained in orbit while the other two made the descent in a small, spiderlike spacecraft called the Lunar Excursion Module. They gathered rocks and samples and took photographs for more than 21 hours.

Five other expeditions followed. These were a little more ambitious. Where the Apollo 11 astronauts didn't stray much more than 100 feet (30.5m) from their lander, other Apollo missions carried a small battery-powered car called a Lunar Rover that allowed them to travel long distances from the landing site. The Apollo astronauts explored lunar **maria**, mountains, craters, and **rills** and brought back valuable information about the formation of both Earth and the Moon. The last humans to visit the Moon landed there in 1972. No one has been back since.

Needed: Pan or box 3 or 4 inches (7.6 or 10 cm) deep, flour, powdered tempera paint, marbles, newspaper

Spread several sheets of newspaper on the floor and place the pan in the middle. Place a thin layer of flour on the pan. Now, standing above the pan, drop a spoonful of flour onto it. What happened? The falling blob of flour made a crater exactly like the ones on the Moon. It may even have a small, central peak just like a lunar crater, such as Copernicus or Tycho. Experiment with different amounts of flour dropped from different heights.

Even though asteroids and meteors are masses of solid rock or metal, the spoonful of soft flour makes a better model than a rock would. This is because the great speeds at which asteroids hit the Moon—tens of thousands of miles an hour—make them vaporize on impact. That is, they act more like a spoonful of flour than a solid rock.

The most striking feature of the Moon is its many craters—thousands of bowl-shaped depressions ranging from just a few feet across to up to 700 miles (1,126 km). Most of these were caused by the impact of meteorites and asteroids. If you were to stand on the rim of one of the largest craters, you would not be able to see the opposite side—it would be over the horizon. Sometimes craters will occur in chains of three or more small, closely spaced craters, which were probably formed by debris thrown from larger impacts. A number of craters are surrounded by **rays**, streaks of bright material radiating out from the crater like a starburst. These were probably created when the explosion of the impact ejected finely powdered material from the surface of the Moon.

The dark patches that form the "man in the moon" are vast, flat plains of old lava. They are called maria (singular *mare*), from the Latin word for "sea," since that's what Galileo, who was the first to observe them through a telescope, thought they were. They were probably formed when huge asteroids punched through the crust of the Moon, allowing vast seas of molten rock to pour out onto the surface. Astronomers have determined that the maria are younger than the surrounding areas, because they have much fewer craters.

The Moon also has high, rugged mountain ranges. Most of them are named after mountain ranges on Earth, such as the Apennines, Alps, and Pyrenees. The lunar mountains are often much higher than their earthly counterparts—some of them rise more than 26,000 feet (7,925 m) above the surrounding plains. The highest mountain in Earth's Alps, Mont Blanc, is just 15,771 feet (4,807 m) high, while Mount Everest, the highest mountain on Earth, is 29,028 feet (8,848 m) high.

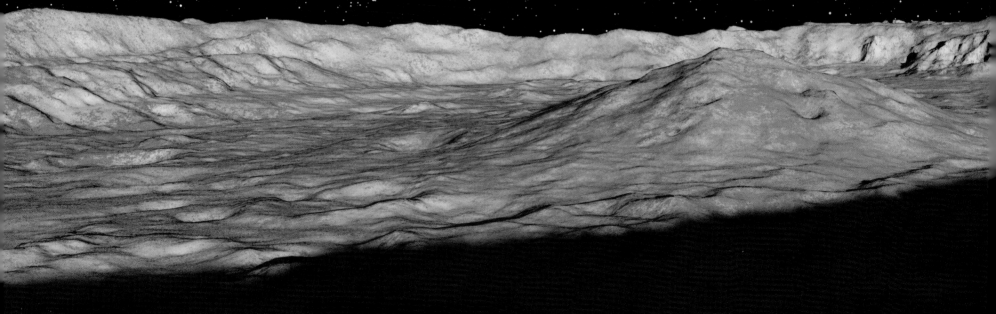

The distant Earth seen from the rim of a giant
Moon crater similar to Copernicus or Tycho

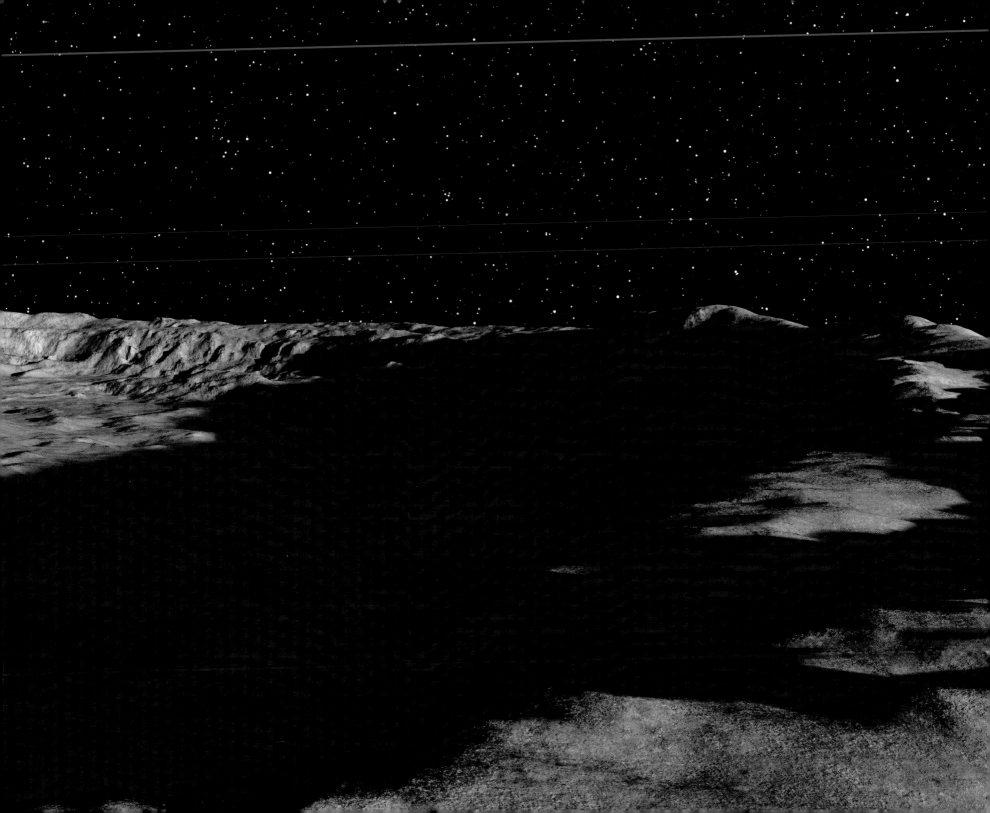

A crater chain is near the center of the large crater at the right in this Apollo 16 photo. This occurs when a comet or meteor breaks up into pieces before impacting. [NASA]

An orbital view of the Moon taken by the Apollo 17 astronauts. A lunar mare, or ancient lava sea, is visible. [NASA]

Boulders in the Taurus-Littrow region of the Moon, photographed by the Apollo 17 astronauts. In the distance are typical rounded lunar mountains, eroded by billions of years of micrometeorites and extreme temperature changes. [NASA]

(73)

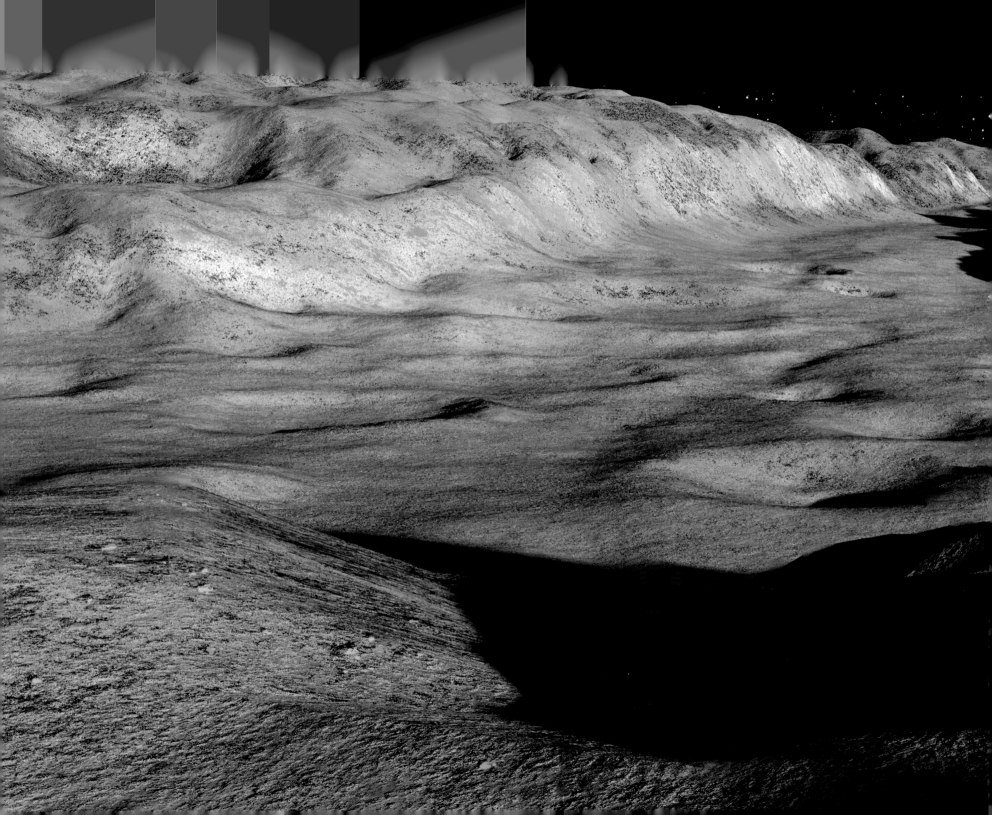

A valley called a rill cuts through the lunar Alps.

Meandering across the surface here and there are rills, sinuous valleys that were probably formed by molten lava in much the same way that water carves out valleys on Earth. Hadley Rille, which was visited by Apollo 15 astronauts, is 75 miles (120 km) long, 1,300 feet (400 m) deep, and up to 1 mile (1.6 km) wide. There are also **scarps**, sloping walls created when sections of the Moon's crust shifted. The most famous of them is the Straight Wall; it is over 90 miles (145 km) long and between 500 feet (152 m) and 1,500 feet (457 m) high.

Perhaps one of the most beautiful views from the Moon is Earth, which would be visible from anywhere on the **nearside**. It never sets, always hanging in the same place in the sky. It is four times larger than a full moon seen from Earth and, because of its cloud cover, much brighter. As the Sun moves through the sky, our planet goes through phases just like the Moon does for us.

Eclipses

As the Moon circles Earth, it occasionally passes in front of the Sun. When this happens an **eclipse** occurs. The midday sky begins to grow dark, taking on a strange, eerie color. The brighter stars appear, and the air grows cool. Birds and animals become quiet, thinking that night is falling; nighttime insects begin chirping. As the Moon blots out the Sun, the outer atmosphere of the Sun, the **corona**, becomes visible in the form of vast, glowing streamers.

Sometimes Earth comes between the Sun and the Moon. When this happens, the Moon passes through the shadow of Earth. During a lunar eclipse, the Moon appears to be a deep

FAST FACTS ABOUT THE MOON

DIAMETER : 2,160 miles (3,476 km)

DISTANCE FROM EARTH: 238,618 miles (384,000 km)

LENGTH OF DAY: 27.3 Earth days

LENGTH OF TIME TO ORBIT EARTH: 27.3 Earth days

Facing page: The Straight Wall is an enormous cliff that stretches for hundreds of miles across the Moon. It was created when a huge block of the Moon's crust rose above the surrounding landscape.

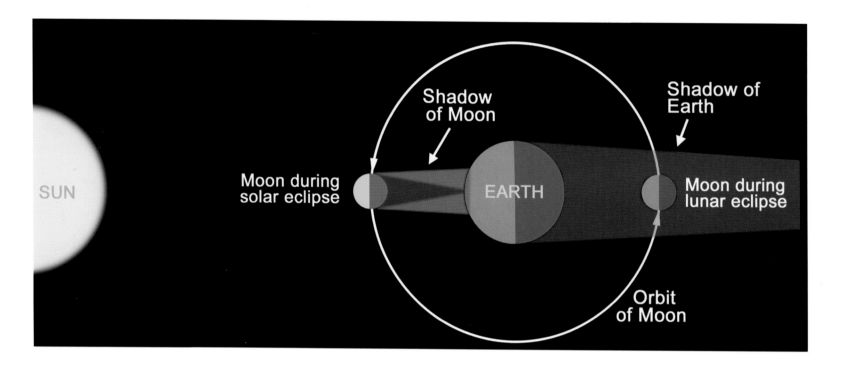

SUN

Moon during solar eclipse

Shadow of Moon

EARTH

Shadow of Earth

Moon during lunar eclipse

Orbit of Moon

Eclipses occur when the Moon passes in front of the Sun, or the Moon passes through Earth's shadow.

Facing page: An eclipse of the Sun by Earth as seen from the Moon: Earth is surrounded by a ring of orange light as the Sun illuminates its atmosphere.

copper color. This is the light that has passed through Earth's atmosphere. From the Moon, Earth would appear to be a black disk surrounded by a thin orange ring—the atmosphere of Earth illuminated from behind by the Sun.

If the Moon orbited Earth in the same plane as its orbit around the Sun, we would have eclipses of the Sun and Moon every month. But the Moon's orbit is tipped, so that sometimes it passes above or below Earth's shadow or above or below the Sun. It is only at those rare times when its orbit crosses the Sun–Earth line that an eclipse can occur.

(78)

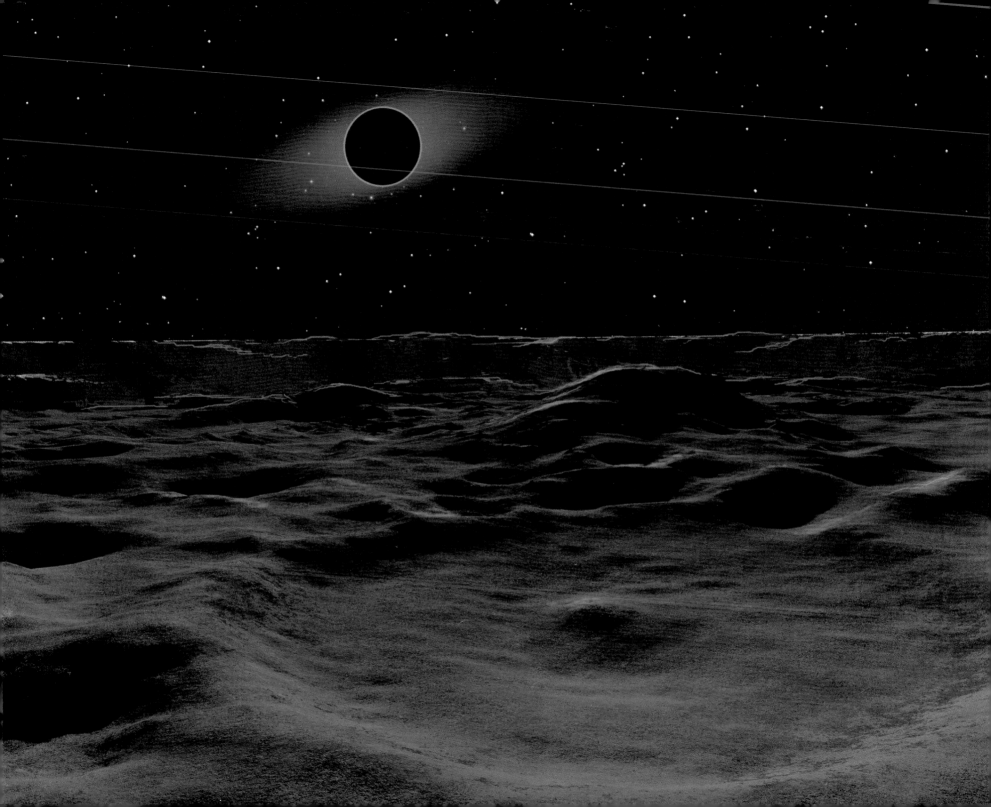

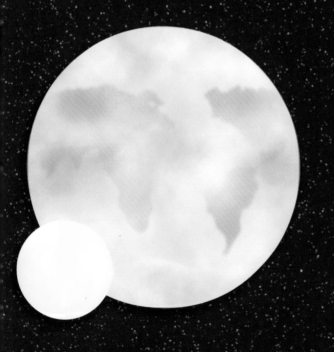

CHAPTER THIRTEEN

THE END OF THE WORLD

If Earth had a beginning, it will also have an end. When most people talk about the "end of the world," what they really mean is the end of human life. We must remember that we have not existed on this planet as a species for very long at all, only a fraction as long as the dinosaurs were around. Perhaps one way in which humans will disappear from the world will be when—millions of years in the future—we have evolved into some entirely different creature, a creature as different from us as we are from one of the tiny, tree-dwelling tarsiers that were our ancestors, or the one-celled organisms all life evolved from.

As we have seen, Earth is not a static body. It is always changing. The continents have not stopped drifting. The Atlantic Ocean is growing wider, and eastern Africa is slowly splitting from the main body of the continent, just as the Gulf of California is growing wider as Baja California moves into the Pacific Ocean. A few hundred million years from now, Earth will look as unfamiliar as it did 200 million years ago. If human beings are still around, they will have to deal with the climactic and geologic changes that will occur.

If a nearby star were to explode into a supernova, it might severely damage Earth's life. A supernova pours vast quantities of deadly radiation into the surrounding universe. And "nearby" does not mean that a star has to be especially close to cause real harm. Betelgeuse, which is 300 **light years** away, could destroy Earth's ozone layer were it to become a supernova. Since we need our ozone layer to protect us from dangerous solar radiation, this would be a catastrophe.

But what of Earth itself? Could anything destroy the entire planet? Certainly. The body that created the Moon when it collided with Earth was nearly large enough to have destroyed the planet. As it turned out, Earth literally absorbed most of the invader. But if Earth were to be hit by something large enough, Earth could be destroyed. Fortunately, there are no unknown bodies in our solar system large enough to destroy the entire Earth, though a small asteroid could certainly do it—and us—a great deal of damage.

Barring accident, Earth should last as long as the Sun itself. And since the Sun is a middle-aged star that is only halfway through its expected life span of 9 billion years or so, there is a lot of time before human beings (or whatever creatures are inhabiting Earth in the distant future) need to worry.

The Distant Future

The Sun's light and heat come from the nuclear reactions that take place in its core. Hydrogen atoms there are **fused**—forced together—to make helium. When this happens, tremendous

The supernova explosion of a nearby star may flood Earth with enough radiation to kill all life on it.

amounts of energy are released. There is an immense amount of hydrogen in the Sun. Even using it at the prodigious rate of 4 million tons a second, it will take the Sun another 6 billion years to finish burning it all.

Unfortunately, things will start happening to the Sun long before it uses up all of its hydrogen. As the amount of hydrogen in the core decreases, fusion will begin to spread outward into the heavier elements in the outer layers of the Sun. The Sun will slowly grow brighter. This is going on now (it's the reason the Sun was cooler and dimmer in the past than it is today) and will continue for another 5 billion years. Three billion years from now, the Sun will be twice as bright as it is now, and the average temperature of temperate regions such as the United States or Europe will rise from 68°F (20°C) to 167°F (75°C).

The Sun will keep on getting brighter and hotter. It will also be getting larger as the ever-expanding core heats the outer layers, causing them to expand. Five billion years from now, the Sun will have become a **red giant** a hundred times larger than it is today. It will have become as large as the orbit of Venus. As the luminosity of the Sun becomes 300 or 400 times greater than at present, Earth's atmosphere will be driven off and the oceans will have long since boiled away. Mountains will melt, filling the dried seabeds with a flood of molten rock. Earth's surface will look as it did at the beginning: a level ocean of boiling lava.

If the Sun keeps on expanding, Earth could enter the outer, tenuous regions of the Sun's atmosphere. Friction will cause Earth to slow down in its orbit, and it will begin to spiral toward the

Facing page: The Sun has swollen into a red giant. The increased heat is melting the surface of Earth.

Sun's interior. It will eventually melt completely, merging with the hot gases at the core of the Sun.

The red giant phase of a star does not last long. Stars have a delicate balance between gas pressures pushing outward and gravitational pressure pushing inward. A star will expand to a huge size if the heat being produced in its interior gets out of control. The expansion caused by this heat will overcome the star's gravity and the star will swell like a balloon. As it runs out of usable fuel, however, the star will begin to lose the war with gravity. It will begin to shrink.

After its red giant phase, the Sun will grow smaller and smaller until it eventually becomes a **white dwarf**, a white-hot sphere no larger than Earth itself. It will be a thousand times dimmer than it is today, and it will keep growing cooler and dimmer. The surface of Earth—what's left of it after the ravages caused by the Sun's red giant stage—will be a dark, barren wasteland dimly lit by a tiny Sun. Any remnants of an atmosphere would be frozen on the surface—the temperature of which has dropped to −359°F (−217°C).

Is there anything that can be done to prevent this from occurring? Probably not, but that's only because solutions are beyond the limits of what today's science is capable of. But who can imagine what humankind—or humankind's successors—will be able to do? There is as much time between now and the death throes of the Sun as there was between the creation of life on Earth and the present day. What could life be capable of in a hundred million years? A billion? Perhaps Earth itself cannot be saved,

Facing page: After the Sun's red giant phase, it runs out of fuel and shrinks into a white dwarf. All that is left of Earth is a barren, burned-out cinder.

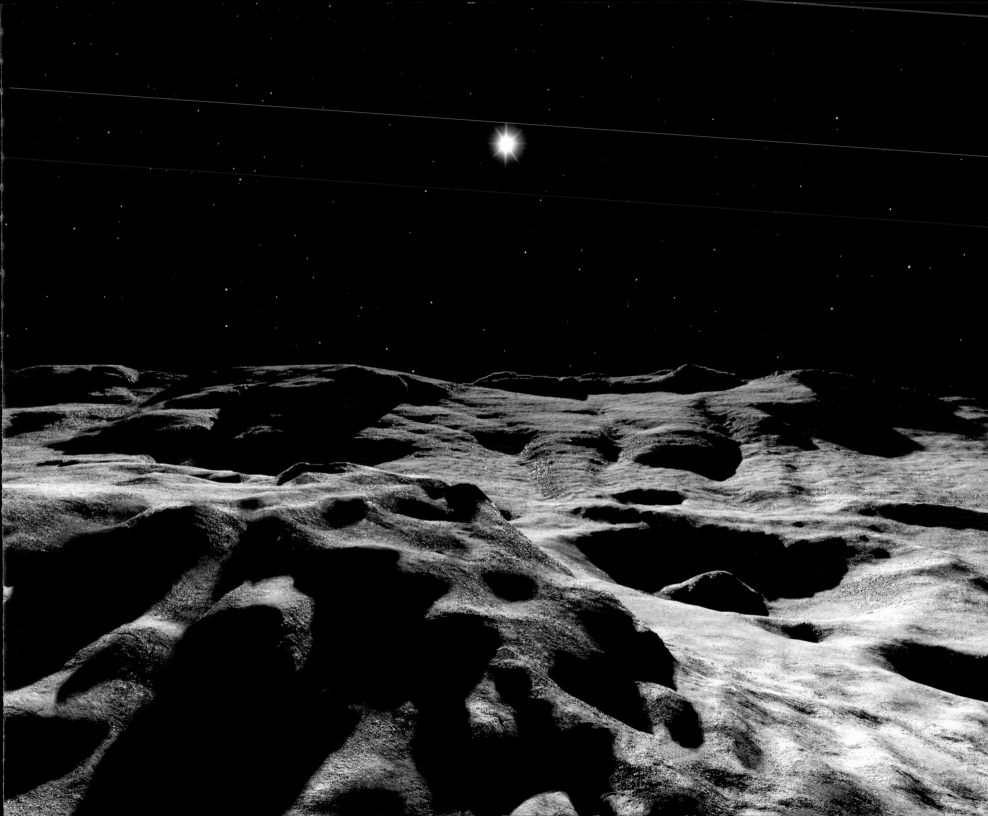

but by that time it may be that life will have spread to new worlds, possibly to some of the new solar systems that have been discovered recently. Perhaps to these beings, the old Earth would only be a dimly remembered legend, a pleasant fairy tale told to their children . . .

A look back at the night side of Earth reveals the continents outlined by the lights of thousands of towns and cities.

accretion—the process by which larger bodies are created by the gradual accumulation of material.

asexual reproduction—a process of reproduction that does not involve the union of cells from individuals of two different sexes. The cell division of an amoeba is a form of asexual reproduction.

asteroid—a rocky or metallic interplanetary body, usually larger than 328 feet (100 m) in diameter.

atmospheric pressure—the weight of the air on a planet's surface.

auroras—glowing light forms seen near the north and south magnetic poles of Earth, caused by radiation from high-altitude air molecules excited by particles from the Sun and the Van Allen radiation belts.

australopithecine—a small, slender form of early hominid. Different varieties appeared primarily in South and East Africa between 1 and 5 million years ago.

body tide—the effect of the pull of gravity of one mass, such as a moon, on another, such as a planet.

brachiopod—a type of mollusk extremely common in Earth's seas in prehistoric times but now quite rare.

climate—the average weather of a certain area over a long period of time.

comet—an ice-rich interplanetary body that, when heated by the Sun, releases gases that form a bright head and diffuse tail.

continent—one of the principal landmasses of Earth, such as North America, South America, Antarctica, Australia, Africa, and Eurasia, separated by the divisions between tectonic plates.

revolution—the movement of one body around another, such as the Moon's path around Earth.

rill—a type of lunar valley.

rotation—the movement of an object around its own axis.

scarp—a steep slope or cliff created when one crustal plate lifts above another one.

seismic—refers to movements of Earth's crust. An earthquake is a seismic event.

sexual reproduction—reproduction in which individuals of a species combine DNA.

solar wind—outrushing gas from the Sun.

stratosphere—the region of the atmosphere above the troposphere and below the mesosphere.

supernova—a very energetic stellar explosion that blows off most of the star's mass, leaving behind a dense core.

terrestrial planet—a planet, such as Earth or Venus, composed primarily of rock and metal.

thermosphere—the outermost shell of the atmosphere, between the mesosphere and outer space.

tide—the effect of an unequal gravitational pull of one object upon another.

trilobite—an extinct arthropod ranging in size from a few inches to 2 feet (60 cm).

troposphere—the lowest region of Earth's atmosphere.

tsunami—an enormous wave created by an earthquake or volcanic eruption.

weather—local, day-by-day changes in the atmosphere.

white dwarf—a planet-sized star of about the same mass as the Sun and with a very high density. It is the last stage in a star's life, as its nuclear fuel has been exhausted.

Books

Beatty, J. Kelly, Carolyn Collins Petersen, and Andrew Chaikin, eds. *The New Solar System*. Cambridge, MA: Sky Publishing Corp, 1999.

Bortz, Fred. *Collision Course! Cosmic Impacts and Life on Earth*. Brookfield, CT: Twenty-First Century Books, 2001.

Downs, Sandra. *When the Earth Moves*. Brookfield, CT: Twenty-First Century Books, 2000.

Hartmann, William K. *Moons and Planets*. Belmont, CA: Wadsworth Publishing Co., 1999.

Hartmann, William K., and Ron Miller. *The History of Earth*. New York: Workman Publishing Co., 1991.

Miller, Ron. *The Sun*. Brookfield, CT: The Millbrook Press, 2002.

Miller, Ron, and William K. Hartmann. *The Grand Tour*. New York: Workman Publishing Co., 1993.

Reynolds, David West. *Apollo: The Epic Journey to the Moon*. New York: Harcourt, 2002.

Schaaf, Fred. *Planetology*. Danbury, CT: Franklin Watts, 1996.

Spangenburg, Ray, and Kit Moser. *If an Asteroid Hit Earth*. Danbury, CT: Franklin Watts, 2000.

Magazines

Astronomy
http://www.astronomy.com

Sky & Telescope
http://www.skypub.com

Web sites

Alpha Centauri's Universe
http://www.to-scorpio.com/index.htm
A good site for basic information about the solar system.

The Big Page of Experiments
http://www.crh.noaa.gov/abr/teacher/experiments.htm
Experiments and projects about the weather; how to create your own weather station.

Destination: Earth
http://www.earth.nasa.gov/
A NASA Web site devoted to Earth sciences.

Earth and Moon Viewer
http://www.fourmilab.ch/earth-view/vplanet.html
Allows the user to view Earth and the Moon from different locations in space.

Earth From Space
http://earth.jsc.nasa.gov/
Thousands of images of Earth seen from the Space Shuttle.

Mr. Eclipse
http://www.mreclipse.com/
Everything about lunar and solar eclipses.

NASA Spacelink
http://spacelink.msfc.nasa.gov/index.html
Gateway to many NASA Web sites about the Sun and planets.

The National Weather Service
http://www.nws.noaa.gov/
Official site of the National Weather Service.

Nine Planets
http://www.nineplanets.org
Detailed information about the Sun, the planets, and all the moons, including many photos and useful links to other Web sites.

Planet Orbits
http://www.alcyone.de
A free software program that allows the user to see the positions of all the planets in the solar system at one time.

Planet's Visibility
http://www.alcyone.de
A free software program that allows users to find out when they can see a particular planet and where to look for it in the sky.

Rocks and Minerals
http://www.connectingstudents.com/themes/rocks.htm
A good source for information on the Internet about geology.

Skywatcher's Guide to the Moon
http://www.space.com/spacewatch/moon_guide–1.html
A complete guide to the Moon.

Solar System Simulator
http://space.jpl.nasa.gov/
An amazing Web site that allows the
visitor to travel to all the planets and
moons and create their own views
of these distant worlds.

The Visible Earth
http://visibleearth.nasa.gov/
A directory of images and anima-
tions of Earth.

Whole Earth Telescope
http://net.iitap.iastate.edu/Obs/
tools.html
Computer tools for observing Earth
and the Moon.

Organizations

American Astronomical Society
2000 Florida Avenue NW, Suite 400
Washington, DC 20009-1231
http://www.AAS.org

Association of Lunar and Planetary
Observers
PO Box 171302
Memphis, TN 38187-1302
http://www.lpl.arizona.edu/alpo/

Astronomical Society of the Pacific
390 Ashton Avenue
San Francisco, CA 94112
http://www.aspsky.org

The Planetary Society
65 N. Catalina Avenue
Pasadena, CA 91106
http://planetary.org

INDEX